CV writing

Before we look at how to structure a CV, you need to make sure you are creating the most visual impact. A poorly laid out CV will be interpreted by a recruiter as potential lack of ability, or even overlooked completely.

Optimise your CV's visual impact

A key point to note is that the top half of the CV is your 'shop window'; it is the first part of your CV viewed on a computer when opened. If in this area you don't start to highlight the skills the recruiter is looking for, or start to imply you are a potential candidate, will they read any further? So, use this space well – having all the key facts hidden away on page 2 will do you no favours.

When writing a CV, many people try and stick to the '2-page rule': that a CV should not be more than 2 pages long. To fit 2 pages, they often shrink the font size and widen the margins. If you are not careful, this turns a CV into a 'wall of words' and makes it unappealing to read.

Interviewers also tend to interview candidates using paper copy CVs so make sure your CV is easy to read when printed by using a good-sized font.

As for the '2-page rule', a 3-page CV is quite acceptable if full of relevant facts and not full of waffle. Page 3 is often where you list courses, training and your qualifications, so do not be afraid to use a 3-page CV.

For some people, such as IT contractors or individuals with a history of working on short term roles, 4 or 5-page CVs may be necessary as you detail the relevant facts.

Finally, to cater for those who are looking to find specific facts about you, make sure transitions within your CV are easy to follow by using spacing between sections and by enlarging the font or using underlining or bold.

Basic CV writing tips

Other factors to consider are:

- Your most recent employer should be on page 1, going backwards in time
- Try not to use jargon, although industry jargon such as JIT is acceptable
- Include 'the numbers' such as 'managed a team of...' or 'responsible for a budget of...' – it is this detail that helps a recruiter measure your capabilities
- Education should be put at the end of your CV. For recent students, however, education should be on page 1
- Although qualifications should be placed at the end of your CV, if a qualification is relevant to your career, reference it on page 1 (covered later)

- Make your CV easy to read by using bullet points
- Choose a modern font to write your CV in
- Be careful with colour and using italic writing. If you do introduce colour, try printing your CV in black and white to see how it looks
- Spell-check your final CV / proofread at 150% normal size
- No need to include your date of birth, although for younger people we often include their age as it helps highlight that they are just starting out
- If sentences in a grammar check show up as grammatically incorrect (green wiggly line underneath) simply leave off the full stop on that line and the green wiggly line will disappear
- Make sure things line up vertically by using the tab spacer. Using the space bar will often resulting in non-perfect alignment = poor presentation
- Finally, with dashes, make sure they are all the same length

Remember, if the job requires high attention to detail and there are spelling errors, things badly aligned, or gaps and spaces where they should not appear, what does this say about your attention to detail?

The 15 second rule / focus your CV to the role

A typical mistake many people make is to write a CV to recount their life story and expect the recruiter to find what they are looking for in the CV. Many people we work with still think a recruiter will spend 3 or 4 minutes appraising a CV, however this is not the case.

With the introduction of online job hunting there has been an increase in the number of applicants and as a result the time recruiters take to screen a CV has dropped. To demonstrate how things have changed, in a 2015 survey in 'The Times' it was highlighted that recruiters appraise the average teenager's CV in 8.8 seconds. If over 19 years of age… this leaps to approximately 15 to 30 seconds.

In both cases we are talking about recruiters dealing with high volumes of applications, but that is in effect, most recruiters working in HR departments or agencies.

Nowadays it is important to write a focused CV bringing to the fore the evidence the recruiter is looking for regarding skills, qualifications and experience, making sure this evidence is quick to find on your CV and stands out, so the recruiter can find it in less than 15 seconds. Once you have gained their attention, they may spend several minutes reading your CV, but the trick is to get their attention quickly, so they will read on.

Our advice is to:

> Treat the job advertisement as an exam question
> Treat your CV as the answer paper

Contents

By doing so, you are writing a focused CV that should mean your suitability for a role is not missed.

If you follow this thought process through you will realise that:

The interview is the spoken or oral exam…

So, if a job advertisement states that you must have 'excellent customer service skills', your CV needs to highlight this skill to the recruiter (if you do have them). But it is not enough to simply state 'excellent customer service skills'. The obvious next question is 'why do you say that?' By not including the evidence to substantiate the statement, the impact of highlighting the skill is lost, so try to support your initial statement with evidence, such as: 'Excellent customer service skills having worked in customer-facing roles for over 10 years'.

Later we will show you how to incorporate these statements into your CV to make the most impact.

Recent students / returners to work

For those new to the job market or returning to the job market after a break, you may be unable to provide work-based evidence to back up your claim to a skill. In this case it might be necessary to highlight the skill required such as 'teamwork', and instead of drawing upon work experience, highlight your ability by providing other evidence, such as being a keen sportsperson or having actively participated in team activities at school / college.

Themed CVs / multiple CV's

Many people often have experience in several areas and can apply for differing job roles. Often, they will try and write one CV to use when applying for these differing roles and expect recruiters to find what they are looking for in the CV. But, as stated earlier, you need to focus your CV towards one type of role.

Ideally then, rather than having one CV where everything is jumbled up, we suggest writing several focused themed CVs. This does not mean dropping other skill areas from your CV, merely bringing to the fore the most relevant evidence for a role.

Graduates / ex-students

Many ex-students are unsure of what they would like to do next. If this is the case, you may need several CVs, one written for each area of employment interest. It is worth spending the time writing these CVs, as by doing so you are demonstrating to a potential employer an interest in an area of employment.

We suggest, however, that you try to focus upon a few job roles and employment sectors, as it may help produce better results.

Tailor your CV

Once you have your CV / CVs written – which may take several hours – it is then important to remember that these are merely templates and need to be further worked on for each application. It is important that your CV is tailored to specific applications and reflects the experience required by the job advertisement.

Even if a job advertisement is like a previous one you have seen, it may have subtle variations and the CV needs to reflect them.
Going back to our analogy:

Job advertisement = the exam question; CV = the answer paper

If the exam question is slightly different, should your answer not be different also?

In the past people did not need to tailor their CV so much, instead sending in a tailored covering letter. Unfortunately, this does not work as well since the invention of email and online applications. Covering letters are often ignored in the first sift, with recruiters going straight for your CV as it should highlight the skills they are looking for.

Also, being practical: 50 applications = 50 CVs; 50 covering letters. How do recruiters cut down their workload by half? Ignore the covering letters.

However, this does not mean you should not send a covering letter. Once past the first screening and at line manager stage, the line managers are interested in what your covering letter says.

Key skill statements / CV profiles

CV profiles started to appear in the 1990s and are on almost everyone's CVs these days. They are paragraphs usually at the top of a CV that try to tell the reader how good you are. Sample profiles can be found on many websites and most get you to highlight soft skills such as:

'A hard-working reliable individual who is quick to learn; has excellent customer service and communication skills; is able to work both independently and as part of a team'

The problem is that most are full of soft skills, very similar in content, and volume recruiters will often not even bother reading them as a result. Would you if they all say the same thing?

In short, then, these generic fluffy profiles do not work and by including them you are wasting part of your 'shop window' – the top half of your CV where you can gain most impact.

If you are going to use such a profile fill it with facts that highlight your skills ability, and most of all, the role you are looking for first, then added detail, and then your soft skills. A good example would be:

> **'Team Leader with over 10 years' experience** managing teams of up to 12 people in both administration and in-bound call centre roles. Strong ability to coach and develop team members to ensure excellent customer service is delivered at all times and staff performance maximised'

You will notice how we have highlighted in bold the role and 10 years' experience. This will stand out on the CV and encourage recruiters to read the profile. The comments about coaching and performance skills relevant to the role and often featured in job advertisements.

Alternatively, instead of using a profile we suggest using the baked beans trick... In the supermarket, you know you have a tin of beans in your hand because in large letters it says 'baked beans'. If you want to know what is in the tin and why it claims to be a tin full of baked beans, you turn it over and read the ingredients.

Use the same trick on your own CV; a headline to identify the role the CV is aimed at and short bullet points underneath to highlight your relevant skills, experience etc.

For example:

Experienced Warehouse Operative / Fork Lift Truck Driver

- **10 years' experience including Goods-In, Order Picking & Packing**
- **FLT Reach & Counterbalance Licences – loading and unloading lorries along with placing stock into the high racking**

The banner headline clearly highlights the role the CV is aimed at. The bullet points then expand on the headline providing supporting facts and answer the questions an interviewer would ask you if you turned up for an interview without your CV.

The headline says an experienced warehouse operative, so if applying for a warehouse role, what questions would the interviewer ask:

- Have you worked in a warehouse before? – Yes, for 10 years
- Doing what? – Goods-in, order picking and order packing
- We also need a FLT operator, what licences do you have? – Reach and counterbalance

Once you have highlighted the relevant experience, it is also important to highlight some of the softer skills required by the role, such as good team player; excellent customer service skills; able to organise and prioritise your workload.

Because these are 'framed' by the hard skills and practical experience and the statement highlighting 10 years' experience, although you might not provide evidence to back up these claims, it is assumed they were developed over the 10 years working in the warehouse.

This means you can add in:

Experienced Warehouse Operative / Fork Lift Truck Driver

- **10 years' experience including Goods-In, Order Picking & Packing**
- **FLT Reach & Counterbalance Licences – loading and unloading lorries along with placing stock into the high racking**
- **Track record of consistently hitting set targets and deadlines**
- **Excellent customer service skills; strong team player**
- **Able to effectively organise and prioritise workload**

Note we use the term *excellent* customer service skills rather than average, OK or reasonable... a CV is there to sell you to get an interview. In retail they always highlight in their adverts excellent customer service skills, so do not be afraid to use the same language when describing your own ability.

If you get the bullet points right, will the recruiter need to read the rest of your CV?

Remember, bullet points are short and punchy statements and should not – unless absolutely necessary – be more than 2 lines long.

Include generic job titles / job title variations / buzz words

CV databases are a tool many job seekers use when job searching. Candidates sourced from them are said to fill well more than 50% of all jobs. Recruiters searching a CV database for candidates will tend to search under generic job titles. This means that, if your actual job title is vague, remember to include on your CV the generic variation. One way to do this is to include the generic version after your actual title in brackets:

> Telephone response handling manager (contact centre manager)

It is also important to include job title variations on your CV. An accounts clerk could also be known as a finance assistant. By including both job titles on your CV you will appear in both searches by a recruiter on a CV database.

When adding in titles remember to include actual job titles rather than refer to a skill area. A recruiter would not search using the term 'administration' when looking for an administrator as many people could have this word on their CV. Only someone who is an administrator is likely to have the job title on their CV.

Another issue people often have is that their job title does not accurately represent what they did. You may easily be rejected for a role because the recruiter interprets what your role was incorrectly. The way to get around this is to highlight the actual role job title in brackets after your real job title:

Account Director (Internal Sales) or Accounts Assistant (Business Analyst)

Finally, in addition to job titles, include the buzz words. These are words recruiters may use to further refine their searches on CV databases. Buzz words could be IT packages; industry jargon; equipment types; or words specific to a role.

As CV database search engines are getting more sophisticated, many have started to rank a CV based upon these buzz words and expected phrases and jargon included on a CV. This can in some cases have a significant impact on where your CV appears in recruiters' CV search results: a CV with the jargon appearing in search results on page 1; without the jargon on page 37 = 370th position with 10 results per page.

Use brackets to highlight specific experience

As part of a role, you may have had experience in an area which you would now like to concentrate on or highlight. Your job title may not imply this experience was part of your role. Again, by using brackets, you can alter the perception of the recruiter about your role:

IT Director (Project Manager)

Thus, highlighting project management was a key part of your job role.

Use the word 'seeking'

If you are looking for a role and have little experience in that area, such as a graduate looking for their first job or if looking to change careers, you cannot include on your CV a statement such as:

Accounts Clerk with 5 years' experience

So instead use the term 'seeking' in your headline:

Seeking a role as an Accounts Clerk / Finance Assistant

By doing so you will appear in search results and highlight to the recruiter that you have thought about the role you would like to do. Next, you need to highlight each skill area required and try to support this with some evidence.

For instance:

Seeking a role as an Accounts Clerk / Finance Assistant

- **Excellent numerical skills with high attention to detail: achieved A* Grades in Maths and Science subjects**
- **Strong team player – played on School Hockey and Netball Teams**
- **Highly committed – passed all course modules first time**
- **Quick to learn and with a passion to follow a career in finance**

You will notice that the last line highlights a passion for finance. Although unsupported with evidence, this says to a recruiter this individual knows what they want to do. A job seeker unsure of their career path may have 10 of these CVs stating a passion for numerous employment areas, but it is only this CV the recruiter will hopefully see.

Structuring the rest of your CV

As previously stated, the top half of the CV is your shop window, so use it to highlight relevant experience. Other expected sections that should be on your CV include:

- Work History / Employment History
- Education
- Training – shows ongoing personal development
- Other information – which can include hobbies and interests; IT Skills; Full Clean Driving Licence etc.

<u>Work history / employment history</u>

When detailing your work history, start by highlighting the company's name, your job titles and the dates of employment so they stand out clearly on your CV – possibly use bold; raised font; or underlining. This is important throughout your CV to make it easy to move between sections quickly and more logical to follow. It also makes your CV easier for a volume recruiter to 'scan read'.

Under each company start by including a brief introduction to what the business does. It is not always necessary to include this introduction as people know who Google are, but which part of Google did you work in?

Next, include a brief introduction or overview of what your role entailed. Imagine you are at a party and someone asks you what you do for a living. Hopefully you would not bore the person, but provide a short and to-the-point overview; ideally 3 or 4 lines long to position your skills and experience.

An error people often make is to launch straight into a long list of duties under their job title that need to be read and mentally added together to understand what they did in a role. By including a brief introduction or overview of your role, it becomes easy and quick for the recruiter to understand what your role involved. It is also easy to alter this brief overview when tailoring your CV to different roles.

Now, underneath the introduction to the business and your role, include achievements rather than duties next. The recruiter has a fair idea from the introduction about what you were doing, so now grab them by telling them how good you were in the role and what you achieved...

Achievements

Achievement can be as simple as: 'consistently hit set targets and deadlines' or 'ensured 100% accuracy at all times when updating databases'.

Achievements often start with an action word and may include the benefit to the business. Often the 'how' is put first, the result second, but if including the business benefit, to make the most impact it may be better to highlight the benefit to the business first – the 'how' second.
So instead of:

'Introduced a number of new working practices that resulted in a £250K saving'

highlight the positive outcome first:

'Saved £250K by introducing a number of new working practices'.

Achievements also do not need to be huge and can be around softer skills:

- Appointed as the main point of contact for key clients turning over £50K+
- Consistently delivered excellent customer service even when working under pressure and to tight deadlines
- Effectively planned my workload to ensure daily targets were met
- Became product champion for the new xxxxx range
- Consistently achieved set targets & SLAs
- Increased sales within 'client A' by 50% over a 3-year period
- Won and developed several new clients, growing the business by over 50%
- Achieved high quality scores in internal audits in relation to customer records
- Ensured all contractual administration and data protection procedures are adhered to as set by SLAs (Service Level Agreements)
- Achieved 100% accuracy when updating files and records
- Effectively coordinated the introduction of a new timesheet logging system
- Increased the customer satisfaction score by over 10% through the introduction of in-house training (management)
- Increased productivity within my team through staff training and introducing a buddying system
- Significantly increased my team's performance through the introduction of new working practices
- Consistently delivered exceptional customer service to site visitors

If you can quantify the results, this helps, but to merely state an overall positive benefit is often enough to impress the reader. To help write achievement statements we have included a list of suggested action words at the end of the CV writing guide.

Achievements as part of your top bullet points

Where you have held very similar roles and your achievements are very similar for each job role, or where they focus on your softer skills, it may be better to highlight how good you are as part of the top bullet points rather than under each role, thus reducing repetition. For example, if working as a customer service advisor, you may highlight for each job as achievements:

- Consistently delivered exceptional customer service
- Effectively resolved difficult customer complaints ensuring client satisfaction
- Organised and prioritised my workload to ensure daily targets were achieved
- Achieved 100% accuracy in database quality audits

These could apply to all the jobs you had, so it may be better to merely introduce the company and your job role, then list duties.

Duties and responsibilities

After your achievements, you need to include your duties and responsibilities. Try to highlight first those that are most relevant for the role applied for. Also, the most important: for a PA diary management and arranging client events should be above filing and updating the CRM system...

Remember to include the detail – you may understand what your role entailed, but the recruiter may not, and you need to state facts and duties.

For example: in accounts roles the individual will often carry reconciliations. If this is not stated on the CV, the recruiter may not realise this was part of your role, however do not go to the other extreme and start including miniscule details.

Education

It is not necessary to list all your qualifications if they are 'old' – in fact many people leave qualifications gained at school off their CV. As the years go by, the qualifications awarded have changed and they can often identify to a recruiter your potential age.

Also, who cares about qualifications over 20 years old, even over 10 years old if not vocational? As stated earlier, education is now often relegated to the bottom of your CV rather than being at the top, but still reference in the top bullet points relevant qualifications that will help support your application.

Recent students, however, should keep education near the top of the CV, unless they have some solid relevant work history.

Shorten your CV / de-ageing your CV

A simple trick to help keep a CV short is to only include full details on job roles you held in the last 10 to 15 years. One way to do this is to summarise older job roles, keeping in the summary and specific experience you feel is relevant as required:

> **Prior to 2000**
> Employed as: Accounts Clerk, Finance Assistant and Junior Accountant

If you have some experience within a previous role, or even if you feel it is important to highlight you worked for a certain employer, include this detail in the summary.

<u>De-ageing a CV</u>

Another benefit of not including the detail with regards older jobs along with the employment dates is that you are also de-aging your CV.

When de-aging your CV, make sure other details are also removed. For instance, dates relating to school / college / university should also be removed. Also as qualifications awarded have changed, it might be useful to also remove reference to the older qualifications. In the UK, polytechnics were renamed universities, so potentially change the establishment details to the new university name also.

Sample CV's and CV headlines

To help pull all our advice together, we have provided on the next few pages a few examples of CVs and CV headlines.

The examples are there to demonstrate how content should be laid out, and the CV samples we are providing are not necessarily the most visually appealing CVs with regard to layout. We therefore suggest you find a CV layout that you like on the Internet, then use our templates as a guide to maximise the impact of the contents.

Sample of a biographical CV

Garry James

Address: 55 Arian Court
                   St Thomas' Drive
                   Any Town
                   Middlesex HA5 4SR   **Email:**   garry@htr-hr.co.uk

Mobile Tel: xxxxxx xxxxxxxxx   **Home Tel:**   0201 xxxxxxxx

Experienced Warehouse Operative / Fork Lift Truck Driver

- **10 years' experience including Goods-In, Order Picking & Packing**
- **FLT Reach & Counterbalance Licences – loading and unloading lorries along with placing stock into the high racking**
- **Good at organising and prioritising workload to ensure targets are met**
- **Strong team player who works well independently**
- **Self-motivated and quick to learn**

(LIST JOB TITLES & JOB TITLE VARIATIONS IN THE HEADLINE TO BE FOUND IN RECRUITERS' SEARCHES ON CV DATABASES; INCLUDE A FEW POINTS UNDERNEATH TO SUMMARISE YOUR EXPERIENCE – TAILOR THIS TO INDIVIDUAL JOBS. TOP HALF OF A CV = YOUR SHOP WINDOW.)

EMPLOYMENT HISTORY

2005 – Present   Roy's Transport and Distribution Ltd
Warehouse Operative (FLT Operator)

Roy's Transport worked for Nisa Food Stores distributing food and non-food products to their retail stores; my role was based in the main warehouse where orders were picked prior to store delivery.
(PROVIDE AN OVERVIEW OF THE BUSINESS – IDENTIFIES TO THE READER INDUSTRY SECTOR / SIZE OF BUSINESS)

For the last 6 years I have worked in the goods-in area unloading lorries using a FLT, also covering in the picking and packing areas during busy periods.
(BRIEF OVERVIEW OF YOUR ROLE AS AN INTRODUCTION)

Achievements:
- Consistently achieved daily targets and picking deadlines
- 100% safety record when operating the Reach Truck in tight racking
- Ensured high levels of accuracy while picking store orders
- (INCLUDE 5 OR 6 AT MOST – AND RELEVENT ONES FOR THE ROLE)

Responsibilities:
- Unloading lorries as they arrive using a counterbalance FLT

- Moving the stock into the warehouse and placing it onto the high racking using a reach FLT
- Scanning the barcodes and logging the stock into the warehouse computerised stock management system
- Carrying out general clean up duties within the warehouse
- Helping to pick individual Nisa Store orders and shrink-wrapping pallets once complete
- Printed off the delivery paperwork to send to dispatch.

2000 – 2005   Self Employed Gardener / Landscaper

General garden maintenance including cutting lawns, clearing rubbish, trimming hedges *(IF THE JOB ROLE IS NOT RELEVANT TO THE TYPE OF WORK BEING SOUGHT, INCLUDE SOME DETAILS BUT NO NEED TO GO INTO GREAT DEPTH. POSSIBLY INCLUDE ACHIEVEMENTS FOR THE ROLE AS AN ALTERNATIVE TO HIGHLIGHT A SKILL YOU DEVELOPED THERE)*

Prior to 2000

Various general labouring and factory jobs

(JOBS OVER 15 TO 20 YEARS AGO ARE PROBABLY NOT RELEVANT TO A NEW EMPLOYER, SO ONE TRICK IS TO MERELY SUMMARISE AN OVERVIEW OF THE JOB ROLES. THIS CAN ALSO HELP TO DE-AGE A CV)

EDUCATION AND TRAINING

1990   **3 A Levels:** Biology, Physics & General Studies
1988   **10 GSCEs:** Including Mathematics and English Language

(IF TRYING TO DE-AGE A CV, REMOVE THE EDUCATION DATES ABOVE)

Courses attended in recent years include:

Health & Safety in the Warehouse
FLT Certification on Reach and Counterbalance FLT Trucks
Pallet Truck basic safety
First Aid (Certified First Aider)
Fire Marshall Training – 2 years as a Fire Marshall at Roy's Transport
Safe Lifting Practices
Food Hygiene NVQ Level 1

ADDITIONAL INFORMATION

Good IT Skills including: Microsoft Word, Excel, and PowerPoint. Also experience of in-house stock management systems whilst at Roy's Transport

I enjoy watching and playing sports, especially football and golf.

Sample CV headlines – for individuals with relevant experience

Fundraising manager

> **Fundraising Manager with 8 years' experience working for Third Sector / Charity organisations**

- Coordinated the raising of funding ranging between £2M and £24M annually
- Excellent ability to develop relationships with local companies and community groups through running events including dinners; conferences; event days; sponsored activities
- Won funding from grant making foundations and private donors through proposals / bid writing – on average submitting 20 applications per year
- Strong team player who has a passion to work towards common goals
- IT proficient: Word; Excel; Raisers Edge; Fluent in French and English

Accounts assistant

> **Experienced Finance Assistant / Accounts Clerk with 15 years' experience (AAT Level 3 Qualification)**

- Worked in fast-moving organisations - SMEs and large companies turning over £250K to £10m
- Sage Line 50 experience includes: Sales Ledger; Purchase Ledger; Credit Control; Payroll; Stock
- Weekly & Monthly Payroll (up to 65 staff) - SSP; Deductions; PAYE; Overtime & Expenses
- Proficient in: SAP; Syspro; Vebra; Sage Line 100; Sage Line 200; Sage Line 500, Excel; Word; PowerPoint
- Good team player, self-motivated and quick to learn

Project manager

> **IT Project Manager with over 16 years' experience**

- Delivered a range of projects across multi-functional areas including: Supply Chain, Production, Finance, Customer Services, Sales, Human Resources
- Track record of delivering complex projects on time and within budget
- Experience with ERP, CRM and portal systems
- PMP Accredited (PMI / PMBOK); Waterfall; Agile; ITIL; working knowledge of Prince2; very proficient in planning with Microsoft Project
- Led teams of up to 50 staff delivering projects across 10 sites and 500 staff
- Controlled project scope, budget, risk, quality and procurement
- Strong Vendor and Stakeholder Management skills

Accountant

Chartered Management Accountant with 20+ years' experience

- Extensive experience of business and financial strategy; financial modelling; and working closely with operational areas
- Key player in the senior management team
- Fully accountable for the day-to-day operations of businesses turning over between £1m and £50m
- Successfully implemented and project-managed several key changes to business operations resulting in increased efficiencies
- Performance-managed teams of up to 8 staff across 3 sites

Administrator / receptionist

Receptionist / Administrator with over 10 years' experience

- Excellent customer service skills, good at building rapport with people
- Well-presented, polite, and a good communicator
- Confident and flexible member of any team, maintaining a high standard at all times; high attention to detail
- Well-organised individual who works well under own initiative
- Works well in demanding and difficult situations – previously employed as a medical practice receptionist
- Bilingual: English and Punjabi
- IT skills: familiar with MS Office and other IT packages (ECDL)

Facilities manager

Facilities Supervisor / Facilities Assistant with over 20 years' experience

- Provided effective support to line managers on facility issues: repairs, office moves, health & safety, postal services, car fleet maintenance
- Awarded the 'Unsung Heroes' award (2012)
- Identified cost savings of over £100K in copy and print costs
- Effectively negotiated with suppliers to bring down cost whist increasing quality
- Co-ordinated and managed all third-party activity and contractors
- Worked to tight and exacting deadlines, ensuring all repairs were carried out within the set timeframes
- An enthusiastic, self-motivated, responsible, reliable and hardworking individual

Sales

Sales Executive / Business Development Manager over 7 years' experience

- **Proven track record of achieving / exceeding targets & deadlines – Top Sales Person Award 2014**
- **80% new business; 20% account management**
- **Sector experience include: utilities; telecoms; training services**
- **Instrumental in launching a new product into the telecoms market in 2013, resulting in sales in excess of €600K per year**
- **Highly organised and able to prioritise own workload**
- **Strong relationship management skills; good at winning and keeping business**

Production / manufacturing

Production Operative / Factory Worker with 20 years' experience

- **Worked on lines producing PCB boards; cable looms; and where hand tools were required in the assembly (hand-soldering etc.)**
- **High attention to detail with a focus on producing high quality intricate items**
- **Able to effectively prioritise and organise my workload; used to working under pressure and to targets / deadlines**
- **Leadership skills having deputised for the supervisor during weekend shifts**
- **Punctual, reliable, and able to work on my own initiative as well as working well within a team**

Housing support officer

Housing Support Officer / Customer Service Advisor with over 17 years' experience

- **Extensive and in-depth knowledge of the social housing sector including legislation, rental agreements,**
- **Excellent communication and customer service skills having been a main point of contact for tenants with property or rental issues**
- **Strong ability to organise and prioritise workload to ensure deadlines are met**
- **Good problem-solving skills, able to effectively resolve tenant issues whilst delivering excellent customer service**
- **High attention to detail; strong team player and well organised**

Retail manager

Retail Manager with over 20 years' experience within a fast-moving retail operation

- Performance-managed teams of up to 15 staff
- Track record of developing a culture of excellent customer service within my teams
- In-depth knowledge of store operations including: recruitment; training; stock management; cash handling; key holder; work schedules
- Increased sales from €20K/week to over €35K/week over a 6-month period
- An inspirational leader who leads by example and achieves results
- NVQ in Retail Management Level 3

IT software engineer

Software Engineer / Software Developer with over 10 years' experience

- Python 3 with object-oriented programming (expert); Bourne and Bash shell scripting (expert); Java and C# (expert)
- Worked within technical teams developing bespoke financial software systems
- Extensive experience with software life cycle and continuous process improvement, including Agile process and Quality Assurance (ISO 9001)
- Worked closely with the sales team and key client contacts to identify and scope software projects and client needs, and to establish SLAs

(Note – With IT CVs, underneath the headline and bullet points we often see listed all the technology the individual has experience of, including operating systems, IT packages used etc. These are listed under the heading 'IT Skills' before the employment details)

Personal assistant / office manager

Over 15 years PA experience supporting Senior Managers / Directors

- Strong office management / personal assistant / human resources background (CIPD Associate)
- Diary management; hotel bookings; stationary ordering; supervising junior staff; facilities management
- Track record of consistently delivering excellent customer service; NVQ Level 3 in Customer Service
- Excellent communication skills both verbal and written
- Good telephone manner, professional, dedicated, flexible attitude
- Strong attention to detail, problem-solving and meeting deadlines

Human resources

HR Generalist / Senior HR Officer / Human Resources Manager with over 10 years' experience

- Extensive knowledge of employment law including: grievance; disciplinary
- Recruitment; Training; Assessment Centre design and delivery
- Talent management and succession planning
- Employee Relations (including Union negotiations)
- Strong manufacturing and commercial background
- Post Graduate Diploma in Human Resource Management; BA (Hons) Human Resource Management & Business IT
- Able to work closely with key managers, often in demanding situations

Customer service

Customer Service Advisor with over 5 years' experience

- Track record of delivering excellent customer service at all times
- High attention to detail, able to prioritise effectively
- Excellent communication skills – face-to-face; telephone and email / letter
- Proficient in Microsoft Office Word; Excel; PowerPoint; Access; Outlook and bespoke software packages
- Multilingual: fluent in English, Bengali, Hindi and Urdu
- Smart appearance
- Calm when under pressure

Teaching assistant

Currently seeking a role as Teaching Assistant / Classroom Assistant / Learning Support Assistant (LSA) – Teaching Assistant NVQ Level 3

- 9 months' current teaching experience with 4 to 11-year-olds
- 4 years' previous experience in schools
- Supported KS1 and KS2 in Literacy and Numeracy
- 1-2-1 and Group Support; including after-school activities
- Special needs support working with: dyslexia; dyspraxia; autism; SEN; ADHD; disability
- Supporting the teacher with arts lessons (highly artistic)
- Excellent communication and pupil engagement skills

> **Process Engineer with 11 years' experience within industrial scale manufacturing**

- ➤ Comprehensive experience in engineering with skills in process improvement, data analysis and solutions advice
- ➤ Master of Engineering with Honours in Chemical Engineering
- ➤ Strong expertise in problem-solving and ensuring tests and trials are easily understood, products are performing properly, and products are reliable
- ➤ International experience having worked across EMEA
- ➤ Excellent customer service skills having worked on client sites including: xxxx
- ➤ Consistently exceeds organisational goals and expectations

Mechanical / electrical engineer

> **HV Construction/Site Manager with 15 years' experience in the installation of Electrical/Mechanical Switchgear**

- • C&G Electrical Engineering 236 Parts 1 & 2;
- • Vast experience in LV-MV-HV systems
- • Scottish Power authorised to WI-1, EN-1& WL-1
- • Worked on: Railways, Power Stations, Offshore Installations
- • Responsible for: Planning, Procurement, Tendering and Installation
- • Excellent working knowledge of Risk Assessments, Method Statements and Audit Assessments
- • Track record of effectively managing employees and sub-contractors in both Electrical and Civil disciplines
- • Ensures all KPIs and deadlines are met
- • Good background in H&S, Quality Assurance, Systems Documentation

When writing your own 'headlines' or profile, a simple trick to identify what to include is to download off the internet 5 or 6 adverts for the role you would like, and analyse the advertisements. Simple read the job advertisements slowly and you will spot repetitions between them, common themes. If they all highlight that they need: a team player; someone who is well organised; excellent customer service skills; and IT skills (Word and Excel) – guess what you need to include as part of your bullet point... exactly these points.

Also, read all the samples CV headlines above for inspiration as to how to showcase your skills. We have included a variety of generic skill phrases within the various sample headlines above that could apply to almost any role.

Recent student / school leaver CV's

The CV examples above are for those with experience. If you do not have this experience in an area, you need to 'paint a picture' of what you can offer the employer instead.

A key part of this is to make sure your CV clearly highlights to the employer that you have a keen interest in a job type, are focused upon the role you are applying for, and where possible provide evidence of ability even if this is from non-work based evidence.

Start by using a headline such as: **Currently seeking a role as a xxx**

This clearly highlights that your application is focused and that you have a conviction to achieve a role as an xxx.

Underneath, use the same bullet point layout as before to highlight the skills required by the role, and as best as you can, provide evidence as to whether it is from school / college / university or from social activities or even short placements.

In addition, you can strengthen your application by including a short personal statement in your CV under the CV heading and bullet points. Unlike a personal profile, a personal statement is used to convey an interest in an area of employment or to explain something away if changing career (looked at next). It is a short sales pitch, and will identify to a recruiter why you are interested in a role.

As an example:

Apprentice application

Seeking an Apprenticeship in Engineering

- Quick to learn, hard-working and adaptable in approach
- Good academic ability: 6 GCSEs grade A-C, including Maths, English and Science
- Currently studying BTEC ICT with Business Studies (distinction grade predicted)
- Good communication skills having experienced the retail environment working with both younger and older people; also assisted with school open days
- Strong team player: Awarded Junior & Senior School Colours for team events
- Active helper in the Sikh community at the local Temple on many Sundays (Sevah)

Personal Statement

I have always enjoyed practical activities including DIY and helping my friends with jobs that need doing. Having thought about a potential career path, I have decided that I would like to follow a career in engineering. I believe I have a mature attitude with the desire to succeed and develop my skills, making me an asset to an employer.

To show how this builds into a full CV:

Sample school leaver CV

Richard James

34 Warburton Road, Epsom, Surrey SU35 9ST
Tel: 07973 XXX XXX   Email: richard@htr-hr.co.uk   Age 18 years
Full Clean Driving Licence – Own transport

Seeking a job in retail as Retail Assistant / Shop Assistant

- **Quick to learn, hard-working and adaptable in approach: good academic achievement with Grades A to B in my A Levels; 9 GCSEs inc. Maths & English**
- **Good communication skills having been on the debating team at school and helping to run weekly meetings and events**
- **High level of commitment and goal-oriented having successfully completed my Duke of Edinburgh Silver Award**
- **Able to deal with people of all ages; worked in Marks and Spencer as part of my school work placement**
- **Strong team player having been awarded School Colours for school team events; keen footballer**

Personal Statement

Having recently completed my A Levels I now wish to start a career in retail. I enjoy working with people which I feel is important in this role along with working as part of a team. My school placement was with Marks and Spencer for a week; this provided me with a good insight into how a shop works; also providing practical skills such as shelf stocking and labelling goods. It also gave me the opportunity to deal with members of the public and an appreciation of how good customer service is so important in retail.

IN THE SPACES ABOVE, YOU NEED TO HIGHLIGHT WHAT JOB ROLE YOU WISH TO FOLLOW, THEN HIGHLIGHT WHAT SKILLS AND EXPERIENCE YOU FEEL YOU HAVE FOR THE ROLE. THE ABOVE HAS USED BULLET POINTS TO HIGHLIGHT COMMUNICATION / ACADEMIC ABILITY / COMMITMENT (TARGET-DRIVEN) AND TEAM WORKING. THE PERSONAL STATEMENT IS USED TO RE-INFORCE YOUR JOB CHOICE BY HIGHLIGHTING A 'DESIRE' TO FOLLOW A CAREER IN RETAIL AND THE INSIGHT GAINED AS PART OF A SCHOOL PLACEMENT.

Education

North Surrey College   **2009 – 2016**

A Levels – Biology A; Geography B; Business Studies A
GCSEs – Maths B; English Language B; English Literature B; History C; Geography C; Science B; Additional Science B; Business Studies C; Design Technology C

© Job Doctor

Work History

ANY WORK HISTORY NEEDS TO BE LISTED, HOWEVER SMALL.

Other Information / Interests

I have completed my Silver Duke of Edinburgh Award and this involved learning new life skills such as cooking and driving a car; numerous physical challenges, camping expeditions, long distance walks in the Lake District and community/voluntary activities.

I have been awarded both Junior and Senior School Colours for team sports including being on the school's 1st team in football. In the lower school I was Deputy School Captain, and in the 6th form House Captain for the School along with being a Prefect.

I enjoy golf, hill walking, and computer gaming in my spare time along with playing football. I was an active member of a local football team for over 6 years, playing in the local football league.

INTERESTS AND OTHER INFORMATION NEEDS TO NOT FOCUS UPON 'SOCIALISING', BUT TRY TO HIGHLIGHT ANY ACHIEVEMENTS OR ACTIVITIES THAT SHOW YOU AS A 'ROUNDED' PERSON = NOT ONLY ACADEMIC BUT THAT YOU OFFER A MORE PRACTICAL SET OF SKILLS ALSO.

What if you have little experience to include as evidence?

As you can see by the layout above, the 'shop window' of the CV is heavily focused on highlighting skills and experience whilst the personal statement is a mini sales pitch. You may not have experience of participating in sports etc., in which case use the personal statement to highlight a keenness / passion for a role:

Personal statement – entry level warehouse role

Having had a week's work experience in a warehouse carrying out general duties, along with always enjoying physical activities such football and the gym, I have decided I would like to follow a career in a warehouse. I offer enthusiasm along with the commitment to do an excellent job. I am flexible regarding hours worked and duties I perform, and will always give 100% to anything I do.

Personal statement – entry level horticulture role

Working as a gardener and having a love for plants, I am keen to follow a career in horticulture. I love working outdoors and get great satisfaction from growing plants. I am quick to learn and will always commit to completing any task that I am responsible for to a very high standard. I am punctual, reliable and well-mannered and would describe myself as outgoing, sociable and a good team player

© Job Doctor

Graduate CV's

Graduate CVs use a similar layout to the sample CV above. The main difference is that you would include under the bullet points and personal statement your education and details about your degree.

If the degree content is relevant to the role applied for it is important to list subjects and options studied as the degree can be viewed as 3 years of subject training. Try not to list just subject headings such as 'Management Accounts' (finance roles). Instead expand on this to highlight areas covered such as – bank and petty cash reconciliations, trial balance, sales and purchase ledger.

You can also include under the top headline reference to your knowledge gained:

Seeking a role as an Accounts Clerk / Finance Assistant having just graduated with a BA (Hons) 2:2 in Business and Finance

- Good understanding of accounts gained during my course including: profit and loss accounts; balance sheets; sales and purchase ledgers
- Strong IT skills: Sage Line 50; Microsoft Excel (advanced); Word; PowerPoint

Underneath the headlines and bullet points next include a 'Personal Statement' highlighting your desire to follow your chosen career path as it strengthens your application – even include words like 'desire' and 'passion'.

<u>Graduates not looking to follow a career related to their degree / general degrees</u>

If the degree is being used as a general degree, you may be better off highlighting what you learned as part of your degree under the degree heading, or aspects of your degree that show personal development. For instance, highlighting a good mark for a 15,000-word dissertation would show literacy skills and imply ability.

In addition, use your personal statement to highlight the fact you studied the subject out of interest and what you feel you gained from your studies. For instance:

<u>Personal statement – graduate seeking a career in retail</u>

Having always been a people person, I studied Psychology at university with the intention of using this as a general degree. Since graduating I have had the opportunity to work as a volunteer in retail; I loved the interaction with customers and thrived in this role. I have therefore decided to follow a full-time career in retail with the aim of progressing into management. I feel I can offer an employer a high level of commitment and a professional attitude.

The following highlights the structure of a graduate CV where they are not looking to follow a career in the subject they studied at university:

Sample graduate CV

Helen Jones
B.A. Hons (2:1) Psychology

Address: 55 Arian Court   **Age:**   23 years
               St Thomas' Drive
               Any Town
               Middlesex HA5 4SR   **Email:**   helenj@htr-hr.co.uk

Mobile Tel: xxxxxx xxxxxxxxx   **Home Tel:** 0201 xxxxxxxx

Seeking a role as a Support Worker / Care Worker having completed my degree in Psychology

- Excellent people and customer service skills, having worked part time in a bar for just under 3 years whilst studying
- Previously supported a family member during a period of illness: washing and bathing; cooking and feeding; general household duties
- A caring and empathetic nature with a desire to exceed expectations
- Hard-working; adaptable and quick to learn
- Strong team player having played on hockey teams for over 6 years
- Excellent IT and written skills

Personal Statement

Having always been a people person, I studied Psychology at university with the intention of using this as a general degree. Since graduating I have had the opportunity to work as a volunteer in an old-age home; I loved the interaction with residents and thrived in this role. I have therefore decided to follow a full-time career in care with the aim of progressing into management. I feel I can offer an employer a high level of commitment, along with a flexible and professional attitude.

EDUCATION

Lancaster University 2013 – 2016   B.A. Hons (2:1) Psychology

Completed as part of my degree a 10,000-word dissertation requiring extensive study; awarded a high 2:1. In addition I undertook several group assignments, acting as team leader on many.

John Westwood School

You may wish to put other qualifications including subjects and grades here, or they can be placed under 'Other Information' at the end of the CV.

EMPLOYMENT HISTORY

Terry Wine Bar   **Part Time Waiter**   **2011 – 2013**

Worked in a busy bar whilst a student. Consistently delivered excellent customer service and often took charge of the bar whilst the owner was at the cash and carry. In addition, I would help cash up at the end of the night and train up more junior members of staff.

OTHER INFORMATION

Excellent IT Skills: Microsoft Word; Excel; PowerPoint; Access; Photoshop; Publisher.

I have completed my Outward Bound Silver Award and this involved learning new life skills such as cooking and driving a car; undertaking numerous physical challenges such as camping expeditions, long distance walks in the mountains and community / voluntary activities.

I enjoy golf, hill walking, and computer gaming in my spare time along with playing hockey. I was an active member of a local hockey team for over 6 years, playing in the local hockey league.

On our graduate template above you will note that employment history has slipped to page 2, but to ensure the reader knows about the bar experience this is highlighted on Page 1 as part of the bullet points at the top.

When you get to employment history and the bar role, the description is not about stacking glasses or taking payments; but about the skills an employer might want.

> 'Worked in a busy bar whilst a student. Consistently delivered excellent customer service and often took charge of the bar whilst the owner was at the cash and carry. In addition, I would help cash up at the end of the night and train up more junior members of staff.'

The description highlights several achievements:

- Ability to work under pressure
- Ability to deliver excellent customer service
- Ability to work as part of a team
- Ability to take a role of responsibility by looking after the bar while the boss was away and training up new staff members
- Being trusted – by her boss allowing her to deputise
- Ability to work as part of a team and support team members
- Also, although not an achievement, good numerical skills

On the CV three short lines, but when used well, highlight impressive skills!

Career changers / sideways move CV's

If you are looking to change career direction, the reasons why you are applying for the role in question are often highlighted in your covering letter. However, with recruiters often not reading your covering letter but going straight to the CV, these reasons can be missed, with the recruiter likely to reject your application as a result.

To get around this, a personal statement can again be used to highlight on your CV why you are looking to change direction or specialise in a specific area:

Complete change of direction from retail to administration

Over the last few years whilst working in retail, I have enjoyed the interaction with people and been heavily involved in the paperwork / administration side of running the shop. I have really enjoyed this aspect of my role and have decided that I would like to move into a more office-based role. I have excellent IT skills along with good written and verbal communication skills. In addition, with vast experience in customer service. I am a strong team player, very organised, and able to prioritise work effectively.

Moving into a project management role after heading an IT department

A major part of my role as Head of IT for the last 10 years has been focused upon delivering projects into the business, and I now wish to specialise and move into a project management role full-time. My role has seen me run project teams of up to 30 across multiple sites, with budgets of between €20K and €200K. I have been responsible for projects full lifecycle including: planning; risk; troubleshooting; and stakeholder management.

Now looking to move to a lower level position

Having been recently made redundant, I have decided that I no longer wish to work as a customer service team leader, and I would like to return to the role of customer service advisor. I have always loved the interaction with people, and this is something I have missed as a team leader. I have excellent people and organisational skills; always aiming to deliver the highest level of customer service. In addition, I have a strong work ethic and an excellent timekeeping record.

By including a personal statement on your CV, you can use it to highlight to a recruiter your desire to have a complete career change. You may not, however, be effectively highlighting your transferable skills – skills gained in one area that are applicable and useful for other roles.

Another CV type which can help an individual change career or help them repackage themselves is a function or skill-based CV. These focus upon and bring to the fore transferable skills.

Functional CV's

As an alternative to a standard biographical CV, another style of CV is a Skill-Based or Functional CV. These CVs focus upon transferable skills and can be far more powerful in convincing an interviewer that you are right for a job role.

The focus is upon skillset first, your job titles second. Rather than be pre-judged based on your job title, and potentially rejected because your job title does not imply you have the right background, they reposition you as a set of relevant skills.

Functional CVs are useful if you are:

1)   A contractor / interim manager, allowing you to summarise areas of ability
2)   Looking to make a total career change, thus repackaging yourself
3)   Wanting to highlight specific skills and experience
4)   Looking to 'slip time' and highlight older experience first
5)   A recent graduate looking to bring evidence together from courses / jobs

A functional CV will summarise your experience under skill headings such as 'Project Management' or 'Customer Service' or 'Teamwork'. This evidence may be not just from one job role, but often from several, even going back several years, with your career history appearing often on page 2 of the CV.

They switch the focus towards your transferable skills.

The problem with functional CVs is that they have to be bespoke: written to the precise job requirements. This is where most people go wrong. Because it takes so much time to keep altering the CV, job hunters produce one CV with a list of skill headings and send it to a recruiter hoping the recruiter will spot the ones they are looking for. They have not got the time. So it is vital to really analyse the job role, identify the relevant skills for the role, and provide precise evidence under those skill headings.

As stated above – if used well functional CVs are very powerful at highlighting to a recruiter that you are right for a role, providing specific evidence to support your suitability for the role rather like when completing an application form.

One thing to note though is that many recruitment agency consultants do not like functional CVs. They make their money by putting round pegs into round holes, and these CVs often highlight your transferable skills, the fact you could be a square peg… something their clients are less likely to pay them a fee for. So, you may be better off writing a biographical CV if using recruitment agencies.

An example functional CV layout would be:

Helen Osmond B.Sc. (Hons) 2:2

Address: 55 Arian Court
St Thomas' Drive
Any Town
Dublin   **Email:**   helen@htr-hr.co.uk

Mobile Tel: xxxxx xxxxxxxx   **Home Tel:**   0201 xxxxxxxx

Operations Manager / Commercial Manager with 10 years' experience

- **Excellent people management skills – managed 100+ staff over a 3-year period in last role**
- **Strong financial experience – worked with budgets up to £1 million**
- **Effective Strategy Manager – managed successful integration of new hardware and software systems, including introduction of major data collection changes within the business, utilising new technologies**
- **Comprehensive knowledge of Project Management with over 5 years' experience**

Project Management

Accomplished project manager with over 5 years' experience working within multifunctional teams of up to twelve staff. Recent projects include:
- IT database implementation: £30K project to implement a new state-of-the-art IT data collection and analysis system. Led a team of 6 staff.
  - Delivered the project on time and within budget
  - XXXXXXX

Summarise in the area all the project management experience you have. Remember it is important to provide a variety of examples to substantiate your ability and provide 'depth and breadth' of experience. INCLUDE achievements!

Change Management

XXXXXXXXXXXXXXXXXXXXXXXXXXXXXXXXXXXXXXXXXXXXXXXXXXXXXXXXX
XXXXXXXXXXXXXXXXXXXXXXXXXXXXXXXXXXXXXXXXXXXXXXXXXXXXXXXXX
XXXXXXXXXX
- Xxxxxxxxx
- Xxxxxxxxxxxxxxxxxxxxx

Strategic Experience

XXXXXXXXXXXXXXXXXXXXXXXXXXXXXXXXXXXXXXXXXXXXXXXXXXXXXX
XXXXXXXXXXXXXXXXXXXXXXXXXXXXXXXXXXXXXXXXXXXXXXXXXX

- Xxxxxxxxxxxxxxxxxxxxxxxxxx
- XXXXXXXXXX
- xxxxxxx

EMPLOYMENT HISTORY

GFLP	2007 – 2009	Business General Manager
Dunlop Research	2001 – 2007	Project Specialist
Tri Changer	1999 – 2001	Operations Manager
J James and Sons	1983 – 1999	Programme Manager

EDUCATION AND TRAINING

1991-1992   University of Cork – B.Sc. in Applied Sciences

Courses attended in recent years include:

Staff Motivation and Targeting; Interpersonal Managing Skills

ADDITIONAL INFORMATION

Member of the Institute of Directors
Proficient in UNIX based SPSS processing systems Quancept & Quantum

HOBBIES AND INTERESTS

Watching and playing sport, especially football and golf, travelling and reading.

Note

As already stated, it is important that these CVs are tailored and written for individual applications. If you write a skill-based CV that is not focused, this can do you more harm than good. After all – as the exam question changes, so should your CV.

Sample of a graduate functional CV

Helen Osmond B.Sc. (Hons) 2:2

55 Arian Court, St Thomas' Drive, Any Town, Dublin
Email: helen@htr-hr.co.uk **Mobile Tel:** xxxxx xxxxxxxx

Seeking a role in retail as a Trainee Retail Manager / Retail Supervisor / Retail Graduate Trainee

- **Excellent customer service and interpersonal skills having worked for over 6 months in a part-time retail role**
- **Good understanding of retail operations including: merchandising; handling payments (cash and card); dealing with deliveries / returns**
- **Able to work well under pressure and consistently deliver an excellent customer experience in busy trading periods such as Christmas**
- **Team player who is quick to learn**
- **IT proficient: Microsoft Word; Excel; PowerPoint; Access**

Customer Service Experience

Working in a customer facing role for over six months, I have learned how to relate to customers and deliver excellent customer service. For instance, whilst…(*summarise in the area all the customer service experience you have. Also, if possible, provide evidence to substantiate your ability and INCLUDE achievements!*)

Retail Skills
(A paragraph outlining your retail skills)

Interpersonal Skills
(A paragraph highlighting your interpersonal skills)

(YOU MAY HAVE 3 TO 6 SKILLS HEADINGS DEPENDING ON THE ROLE)

EMPLOYMENT HISTORY

GFLP	2012 – 2014	Retail Assistant
Dunlop Research	2011 – 2011	Temporary Admin Work

EDUCATION AND TRAINING

2015   University of Cork – B.Sc. in Applied Sciences 2:2

ADDITIONAL INFORMATION

Include detail as per previous CV examples

Creative CV's

Individuals from creative industries, such as: web developers; graphic designers; architects etc. can greatly enhance their CV by including samples of their drawings / work. Rather than use sketches as a watermark under your CVs content or including the diagrams within the body of the CV, we advise a cover sheet at the front of your CV.

On the cover sheet, include your name and your headline, then six samples of your work sized to be easily seen, detail clear, and chosen to demonstrate either your specialism in a specific area or your overall experience.

As an example an architectural individual may include drawings of housing designs; industrial units; schools; hospitals; refurbishments; or renovation projects. Choose these items carefully and ensure there is clarity in the drawings / sketches / diagrams. To help, label each one so a recruiter can quickly identify what they are.

For cartoonists / game designers / video and other associated creative industries, this is not so easy. In this case, place a show reel on Internet sites such as Vimeo (www.vimeo.com) and include the web link on your CV.

As an alternative, build your own website to feature your productions. One company we recommend to host a website is 1&1 (www.1and1.com in Ireland and for the UK www.1and1.co.uk). They provide cheap web hosting and excellent website templates.

Academic CV's

Those looking for academic roles are often asked to provide a CV with a covering letter when applying. If you are looking at these roles, please IGNORE all the advice we have provided regarding CV layout, structure, and including CV bullet points / headlines / personal statements.

Yes – ignore …

Academic CVs are based upon a CV format that has not changed over the last 30 years, if not longer. Education is featured at the top of the CV, areas of research often next, and at the end of the CV publications and patients. Somewhere in the middle, career history is featured.

If you are looking at roles in this sector we suggest contacting a university or college careers departments to obtain sample CV layouts.

Full time roles are usually filled via an application form process, but if using a CV, the most important part of your application is your covering letter. In your covering letter it is essential to highlight your suitability for the academic research or teaching role question, in detail and often great depth, utilising examples where possible.

Phrases and words for CV's

The language used in a CV can really help to 'sell' you and project a certain image. For instance, "Performance-managed twenty staff..." sounds far more impressive than "Managed twenty staff..." Here are some words that can be incorporated into your CV to emphasise your abilities:

Accountable	Achieved	Adaptable	Ambitious
Analytical	Articulate	Capable	Challenging
Committed	Competitive	Concise	Confident
Conscientious	Consistent	Consultative	Creative
Decisive	Dedicated	Determined	Diplomatic
Efficient	Empowering	Entrepreneurial	Enthusiastic
Fair	Flexible	Friendly	Genuine
Helpful	Honest	Imaginative	Independent
Influential	Innovative	Inspirational	Inventive
Knowledgeable	Logical	Loyal	Motivational
Objective	Optimistic	Organised	Originate
Perceptive	Perfectionist	Persistent	Persuasive
Pioneering	Positive	Practical	Pragmatic
Precise	Professional	Proactive	Performance
Realistic	Reconcile	Reliable	Resolved
Resourceful	Responsible	Risk	Scientific
Self-Reliant	Shaped	Sincere	Supportive
Systematic	Thoughtful	Tolerant	Tenacious
Versatile	Visionary		

When highlighting achievements, by starting the achievement with an 'action' word you can emphasise the achievement. Words such as:

Accomplished	Attained	Achieved	Analysed
Created	Calculated	Consolidated	Conceived
Conducted	Converted	Designed	Directed
Defined	Developed	Ensured	Established
Engineered	Eradicated	Exceeded	Expanded
Enhanced	Executed	Evaluated	Founded
Generated	Headed	Halved	Highlighted
Instigated	Introduced	Inspired	Initiated
Led	Launched	Liaise	Lowered
Met	Modified	Minimised	Motivated
Negotiated	Originated	Overcame	Outlined
Organised	Optimised	Performance	Piloted
Performed	Proposed	Promoted	Reorganised
Restructured	Revamped	Recommended	Resolved
Retained	Specified	Shaped	Saved
Streamlined	Strengthened	Set up	Solved
Scheduled	Stimulated	Supported	Transformed

Application forms

CVs tend to often allude to a skill and tend to be brief overviews of your abilities and capabilities. Application forms are the opposite, asking you to provide lots of detail and often examples to demonstrate your ability and experience in an area.

The first thing to note is that, when filling application forms in, read the instructions and follow them precisely. If it says use a black pen, use a black pen or you might just be rejected for the colour of the ink – it does happen.

Print clearly, use a dictionary, and if online, try to print the form off before completing it, giving you time to think about what you are going to type in.

So how do you fill them in?

The majority of the form is usually simple to complete, asking for personal, employment and educational details. The most important area is where you are asked to provide supporting evidence.

If the application form has a number of individual boxes to fill in, read the question carefully and enter evidence into each. Most application forms have one large empty supporting evidence box, so when completing it:

1. Use the person specification as the basis for your statement
2. Treat each point on the person specification as a separate exam question
3. Highlight each point in turn in the supporting evidence box – you can even copy the language from the specification over
4. Now provide an overview of how you met the requirement; next specific detail; and potentially examples to help provide depth and support your application

If you are asked to use additional sheets as required, often they expect this. This box may be scored like an exam. If not enough evidence = lower score.

One way to gain extra marks is to provide examples to support your application, and when recounting these examples we suggest using the S.T.A.R. technique as it will help to structure your evidence:

S = Situation – Describe the scene and this MUST be done well
T = Tasks – Identify any tasks involved and their importance
A = Actions – Your actions
R = Results – The benefit/results you achieved

Too many people do just an **A.R**... but setting the scene is critical to be judged properly. Ideally, then, think of the example you provide being marked:

The ST = 4 marks; A = 4 marks; R = 2 marks

(A variation on this is **I.P.A.R.**   I=Introduction; **P**=Problem; **A**=Action; **R**=Results)

© Job Doctor

Good Luck with the job hunting!

Extra Help and Support

Extra help and support

If you are struggling or feel you would benefit from extra help in areas such as CV writing, completing application forms, preparing for an interview, preparing for a presentation, preparing for an assessment centre or effective job hunting, we provide both remote support (via Skype and telephone) and individual face-to-face support.

Remote (Skype) support is purchased by the hour and available in the UK, Ireland and internationally.

Face-to-face support is provided on a 1-2-1 basis (UK and Republic of Ireland only)

For more information, please visit: www.job-doctor.com
Or email us at: info@job-doctor.com

Disclaimer

To the full extent permissible by law, Job Doctor disclaims all responsibility for any damages or losses (including, without limitation, financial loss, damages for loss in business projects, loss of profit or other consequential losses) arising in contract, tort or otherwise from the use of this guide, or from any action or decision taken as a result of using information and advice contained within the guide.

If any of these terms should be determined to be illegal, invalid or otherwise unenforceable by reason of the laws of any state or country in which these terms are intended to be effective, then to the extent and within the jurisdiction in which that term is illegal, invalid or enforceable, it shall be severed and deleted from the clause concerned and the remaining terms and conditions shall survive, remain in full force and effect and continue to be binding and enforceable.

These Terms and Conditions shall be governed by and construed in accordance with English law. Disclaimer issued – 17th November 2017.

CPSIA information can be obtained
at www.ICGtesting.com
Printed in the USA
LVOW09s1932260318
571187LV00010B/570/P